ICC Uniform Customs
and Practice for

Documentary Credits 2007 REVISION

Implementation Date
July 1, 2007

The Uniform Customs and Practice for Documentary Credits were first published by ICC in 1933. Revised versions were issued in 1951, 1962, 1974, 1983 and 1993.

This revision was adopted by the ICC Executive Board in November 2006 and first published as ICC Publication No. 600 in December 2006.

The English language version of the Uniform Customs and Practice for Documentary Credits provides the official text of the rules. The titles provided for the articles are for reference only.

The official French translation is also published by ICC SERVICES, Publications Department. Translations in other languages and bilingual versions may be available from ICC national committees. Please visit www.iccwbo.org for a full list of national committees.

Copyright © 2006
International Chamber of Commerce

All rights reserved. This collective work was initiated by ICC which holds all rights as defined by the French Code of Intellectual Property. No part of this work may be reproduced or copied in any form or by any means – graphic, electronic, or mechanical, including photocopying, scanning, recording, taping, or information retrieval systems – without the written permission of ICC SERVICES, Publications Department.

Reprinted January 2007

ICC SERVICES
Publications Department
38, cours Albert 1er
75008 Paris – France
www.iccbooks.com

ICC Publication No. 600
ISBN-10: 92-842-1257-X
ISBN-13: 978-92-842-1257-6

Foreword

This revision of the Uniform Customs and Practice for Documentary Credits (commonly called "UCP") is the sixth revision of the rules since they were first promulgated in 1933. It is the fruit of more than three years of work by the International Chamber of Commerce's (ICC) Commission on Banking Technique and Practice.

ICC, which was established in 1919, had as its primary objective facilitating the flow of international trade at a time when nationalism and protectionism posed serious threats to the world trading system. It was in that spirit that the UCP were first introduced – to alleviate the confusion caused by individual countries' promoting their own national rules on letter of credit practice. The objective, since attained, was to create a set of contractual rules that would establish uniformity in that practice, so that practitioners would not have to cope with a plethora of often conflicting national regulations. The universal acceptance of the UCP by practitioners in countries with widely divergent economic and judicial systems is a testament to the rules' success.

It is important to recall that the UCP represent the work of a private international organization, not a governmental body. Since its inception, ICC has insisted on the central role of self-regulation in business practice. These rules, formulated entirely by experts in the private sector, have validated that approach. The UCP remain the most successful set of private rules for trade ever developed.

A range of individuals and groups contributed to the current revision, which is entitled "UCP 600". These include the UCP Drafting Group, which sifted through more than 5000 individual comments before arriving at this consensus text; the UCP Consulting Group, consisting of members from more than 25 countries, which served as the advisory body reacting to and proposing changes to the various drafts; the more than 400 members of the ICC Commission on Banking Technique and Practice, who made pertinent suggestions for changes in the text; and ICC national committees worldwide, which took an active role in consolidating comments from their members. ICC also expresses its gratitude to practitioners in the transport and insurance industries, whose perceptive suggestions honed the final draft.

Guy Sebban
Secretary General
International Chamber of Commerce

© 2006 International Chamber of Commerce

Contents

© 2006 International Chamber of Commerce

© 2006 International Chamber of Commerce

ICC Uniform Customs and Practice for Documentary Credits

Introduction

In May 2003, the International Chamber of Commerce authorized the ICC Commission on Banking Technique and Practice (Banking Commission) to begin a revision of the *Uniform Customs and Practice for Documentary Credits*, ICC Publication No. 500.

As with other revisions, the general objective was to address developments in the banking, transport and insurance industries. Additionally, there was a need to look at the language and style used in the UCP to remove wording that could lead to inconsistent application and interpretation.

When work on the revision started, a number of global surveys indicated that, because of discrepancies, approximately 70% of documents presented under letters of credit were being rejected on first presentation. This obviously had, and continues to have, a negative effect on the letter of credit being seen as a means of payment and, if unchecked, could have serious implications for maintaining or increasing its market share as a recognized means of settlement in international trade. The introduction by banks of a discrepancy fee has highlighted the importance of this issue, especially when the underlying discrepancies have been found to be dubious or unsound. Whilst the number of cases involving litigation has not grown during the lifetime of UCP 500, the introduction of the ICC's Documentary Credit Dispute Resolution Expertise Rules (DOCDEX) in October 1997 (subsequently revised in March 2002) has resulted in more than 60 cases being decided.

To address these and other concerns, the Banking Commission established a Drafting Group to revise UCP 500. It was also decided to create a second group, known as the Consulting Group, to review and advise on early drafts submitted by the Drafting Group. The Consulting Group, made up of over 40 individuals from 26 countries, consisted of banking and transport industry experts. Ably co-chaired by John Turnbull, Deputy General Manager, Sumitomo Mitsui Banking Corporation Europe Ltd, London and Carlo Di Ninni, Adviser, Italian Bankers Association, Rome, the Consulting Group provided valuable input to the Drafting Group prior to release of draft texts to ICC national committees.

The Drafting Group began the review process by analyzing the content of the official Opinions issued by the Banking Commission under UCP 500. Some 500 Opinions were reviewed to assess

© 2006 International Chamber of Commerce

whether the issues involved warranted a change in, an addition to or a deletion of any UCP article. In addition, consideration was given to the content of the four Position Papers issued by the Commission in September 1994, the two Decisions issued by the Commission (concerning the introduction of the euro and the determination of what constituted an original document under UCP 500 sub-article 20(b)) and the Decisions issued in DOCDEX cases.

During the revision process, notice was taken of the considerable work that had been completed in creating the *International Standard Banking Practice for the Examination of Documents under Documentary Credits* (ISBP), ICC Publication No. 645. This publication has evolved into a necessary companion to the UCP for determining compliance of documents with the terms of letters of credit. It is the expectation of the Drafting Group and the Banking Commission that the application of the principles contained in the ISBP, including subsequent revisions thereof, will continue during the time UCP 600 is in force. At the time UCP 600 is implemented, there will be an updated version of the ISBP to bring its contents in line with the substance and style of the new rules.

The four Position Papers issued in September 1994 were issued subject to their application under UCP 500; therefore, they will not be applicable under UCP 600. The essence of the Decision covering the determination of an original document has been incorporated into the text of UCP 600. The outcome of the DOCDEX cases were invariably based on existing ICC Banking Commission Opinions and therefore contained no specific issues that required addressing in these rules.

One of the structural changes to the UCP is the introduction of articles covering definitions (article 2) and interpretations (article 3). In providing definitions of roles played by banks and the meaning of specific terms and events, UCP 600 avoids the necessity of repetitive text to explain their interpretation and application. Similarly, the article covering interpretations aims to take the ambiguity out of vague or unclear language that appears in letters of credit and to provide a definitive elucidation of other characteristics of the UCP or the credit.

During the course of the last three years, ICC national committees were canvassed on a range of issues to determine their preferences on alternative texts submitted by the Drafting Group. The results of this exercise and the considerable input from national committees on individual items in the text is reflected in the content of UCP 600.

© 2006 International Chamber of Commerce

The Drafting Group considered, not only the current practice relative to the documentary credit, but also tried to envisage the future evolution of that practice.

This revision of the UCP represents the culmination of over three years of extensive analysis, review, debate and compromise amongst the various members of the Drafting Group, the members of the Banking Commission and the respective ICC national committees. Valuable comment has also been received from the ICC Commission on Transport and Logistics, the Commission on Commercial Law and Practice and the Committee on Insurance.

It is not appropriate for this publication to provide an explanation as to why an article has been worded in such a way or what is intended by its incorporation into the rules. For those interested in understanding the rationale and interpretation of the articles of UCP 600, this information will be found in the *Commentary* to the rules, ICC Publication No. 680, which represents the Drafting Group's views.

On behalf of the Drafting Group, I would like to extend our deep appreciation to the members of the Consulting Group, ICC national committees and members of the Banking Commission for their professional comments and their constructive participation in this process.

Special thanks are due to the members of the Drafting Group and their institutions, who are listed below in alphabetical order.

Nicole Keller – Vice President, Service International Products, Dresdner Bank AG, Frankfurt, Germany; Representative to the ICC Commission on Banking Technique and Practice;

Laurence Kooy – Legal Adviser, BNP Paribas, Paris, France; Representative to the ICC Commission on Banking Technique and Practice;

Katja Lehr – Business Manager, Trade Services Standards, SWIFT, La Hulpe, Belgium, then Vice President, Membership Representation, International Financial Services Association, New Jersey, USA; Representative to the ICC Commission on Banking Technique and Practice;

Ole Malmqvist – Vice President, Danske Bank, Copenhagen, Denmark; Representative to the ICC Commission on Banking Technique and Practice;

© 2006 International Chamber of Commerce

Paul Miserez – Head of Trade Finance Standards, SWIFT, La Hulpe, Belgium; Representative to the ICC Commission on Banking Technique and Practice;

René Mueller – Director, Credit Suisse, Zurich, Switzerland; Representative to the ICC Commission on Banking Technique and Practice;

Chee Seng Soh – Consultant, Association of Banks in Singapore, Singapore; Representative to the ICC Commission on Banking Technique and Practice;

Dan Taylor – President and CEO, International Financial Services Association, New Jersey, USA; Vice Chairman, ICC Commission on Banking Technique and Practice;

Alexander Zelenov – Director, Vnesheconombank, Moscow, Russia; Vice Chairman, ICC Commission on Banking Technique and Practice;

Ron Katz – Policy Manager, ICC Commission on Banking Technique and Practice, International Chamber of Commerce, Paris, France.

The undersigned had the pleasure of chairing the Drafting Group.

It was through the generous giving of their knowledge, time and energy that this revision was accomplished so successfully. As Chair of the Drafting Group, I would like to extend to them and to their institutions my gratitude for their contribution, for a job well done and for their friendship. I would also like to extend my sincere thanks to the management of ABN AMRO Bank N.V., for their understanding, patience and support during the course of this revision process.

Gary Collyer
Corporate Director,
ABN AMRO Bank N.V., London, UK
and Technical Adviser to the ICC Commission
on Banking Technique and Practice

November 2006

© 2006 International Chamber of Commerce

ARTICLE 1

Application of UCP

The *Uniform Customs and Practice for Documentary Credits, 2007 Revision*, ICC Publication No. 600 ("UCP") are rules that apply to any documentary credit ("credit") (including, to the extent to which they may be applicable, any standby letter of credit) when the text of the credit expressly indicates that it is subject to these rules. They are binding on all parties thereto unless expressly modified or excluded by the credit.

ARTICLE 2

Definitions

For the purpose of these rules:

Advising bank means the bank that advises the credit at the request of the issuing bank.

Applicant means the party on whose request the credit is issued.

Banking day means a day on which a bank is regularly open at the place at which an act subject to these rules is to be performed.

Beneficiary means the party in whose favour a credit is issued.

Complying presentation means a presentation that is in accordance with the terms and conditions of the credit, the applicable provisions of these rules and international standard banking practice.

Confirmation means a definite undertaking of the confirming bank, in addition to that of the issuing bank, to honour or negotiate a complying presentation.

Confirming bank means the bank that adds its confirmation to a credit upon the issuing bank's authorization or request.

Credit means any arrangement, however named or described, that is irrevocable and thereby constitutes a definite undertaking of the issuing bank to honour a complying presentation.

© 2006 International Chamber of Commerce

Honour means:

a. to pay at sight if the credit is available by sight payment.

b. to incur a deferred payment undertaking and pay at maturity if the credit is available by deferred payment.

c. to accept a bill of exchange ("draft") drawn by the beneficiary and pay at maturity if the credit is available by acceptance.

Issuing bank means the bank that issues a credit at the request of an applicant or on its own behalf.

Negotiation means the purchase by the nominated bank of drafts (drawn on a bank other than the nominated bank) and/or documents under a complying presentation, by advancing or agreeing to advance funds to the beneficiary on or before the banking day on which reimbursement is due to the nominated bank.

Nominated bank means the bank with which the credit is available or any bank in the case of a credit available with any bank.

Presentation means either the delivery of documents under a credit to the issuing bank or nominated bank or the documents so delivered.

Presenter means a beneficiary, bank or other party that makes a presentation.

ARTICLE 3

Interpretations

For the purpose of these rules:

Where applicable, words in the singular include the plural and in the plural include the singular.

A credit is irrevocable even if there is no indication to that effect.

A document may be signed by handwriting, facsimile signature, perforated signature, stamp, symbol or any other mechanical or electronic method of authentication.

A requirement for a document to be legalized, visaed, certified or similar will be satisfied by any signature, mark, stamp or label on the document which appears to satisfy that requirement.

© 2006 International Chamber of Commerce

Branches of a bank in different countries are considered to be separate banks.

Terms such as "first class", "well known", "qualified", "independent", "official", "competent" or "local" used to describe the issuer of a document allow any issuer except the beneficiary to issue that document.

Unless required to be used in a document, words such as "prompt", "immediately" or "as soon as possible" will be disregarded.

The expression "on or about" or similar will be interpreted as a stipulation that an event is to occur during a period of five calendar days before until five calendar days after the specified date, both start and end dates included.

The words "to", "until", "till", "from" and "between" when used to determine a period of shipment include the date or dates mentioned, and the words "before" and "after" exclude the date mentioned.

The words "from" and "after" when used to determine a maturity date exclude the date mentioned.

The terms "first half" and "second half" of a month shall be construed respectively as the 1st to the 15th and the 16th to the last day of the month, all dates inclusive.

The terms "beginning", "middle" and "end" of a month shall be construed respectively as the 1st to the 10th, the 11th to the 20th and the 21st to the last day of the month, all dates inclusive.

© 2006 International Chamber of Commerce

Article 4

Credits v. Contracts

a. A credit by its nature is a separate transaction from the sale or other contract on which it may be based. Banks are in no way concerned with or bound by such contract, even if any reference whatsoever to it is included in the credit. Consequently, the undertaking of a bank to honour, to negotiate or to fulfil any other obligation under the credit is not subject to claims or defences by the applicant resulting from its relationships with the issuing bank or the beneficiary.

A beneficiary can in no case avail itself of the contractual relationships existing between banks or between the applicant and the issuing bank.

b. An issuing bank should discourage any attempt by the applicant to include, as an integral part of the credit, copies of the underlying contract, proforma invoice and the like.

Article 5

Documents v. Goods, Services or Performance

Banks deal with documents and not with goods, services or performance to which the documents may relate.

Article 6

Availability, Expiry Date and Place for Presentation

a. A credit must state the bank with which it is available or whether it is available with any bank. A credit available with a nominated bank is also available with the issuing bank.

b. A credit must state whether it is available by sight payment, deferred payment, acceptance or negotiation.

c. A credit must not be issued available by a draft drawn on the applicant.

d. i. A credit must state an expiry date for presentation. An expiry date stated for honour or negotiation will be deemed to be an expiry date for presentation.

© 2006 International Chamber of Commerce

ii. The place of the bank with which the credit is available is the place for presentation. The place for presentation under a credit available with any bank is that of any bank. A place for presentation other than that of the issuing bank is in addition to the place of the issuing bank.

e. Except as provided in sub-article 29 (a), a presentation by or on behalf of the beneficiary must be made on or before the expiry date.

Article 7

Issuing Bank Undertaking

a. Provided that the stipulated documents are presented to the nominated bank or to the issuing bank and that they constitute a complying presentation, the issuing bank must honour if the credit is available by:

i. sight payment, deferred payment or acceptance with the issuing bank;

ii. sight payment with a nominated bank and that nominated bank does not pay;

iii. deferred payment with a nominated bank and that nominated bank does not incur its deferred payment undertaking or, having incurred its deferred payment undertaking, does not pay at maturity;

iv. acceptance with a nominated bank and that nominated bank does not accept a draft drawn on it or, having accepted a draft drawn on it, does not pay at maturity;

v. negotiation with a nominated bank and that nominated bank does not negotiate.

b. An issuing bank is irrevocably bound to honour as of the time it issues the credit.

c. An issuing bank undertakes to reimburse a nominated bank that has honoured or negotiated a complying presentation and forwarded the documents to the issuing bank. Reimbursement for the amount of a complying presentation under a credit available by acceptance or deferred payment is due at maturity, whether or not the nominated bank prepaid or purchased before maturity. An issuing bank's undertaking to reimburse a nominated bank is independent of the issuing bank's undertaking to the beneficiary.

© 2006 International Chamber of Commerce

Article 8

Confirming Bank Undertaking

a. Provided that the stipulated documents are presented to the confirming bank or to any other nominated bank and that they constitute a complying presentation, the confirming bank must:

i. honour, if the credit is available by

a) sight payment, deferred payment or acceptance with the confirming bank;

b) sight payment with another nominated bank and that nominated bank does not pay;

c) deferred payment with another nominated bank and that nominated bank does not incur its deferred payment undertaking or, having incurred its deferred payment undertaking, does not pay at maturity;

d) acceptance with another nominated bank and that nominated bank does not accept a draft drawn on it or, having accepted a draft drawn on it, does not pay at maturity;

e) negotiation with another nominated bank and that nominated bank does not negotiate.

ii. negotiate, without recourse, if the credit is available by negotiation with the confirming bank.

b. A confirming bank is irrevocably bound to honour or negotiate as of the time it adds its confirmation to the credit.

c. A confirming bank undertakes to reimburse another nominated bank that has honoured or negotiated a complying presentation and forwarded the documents to the confirming bank. Reimbursement for the amount of a complying presentation under a credit available by acceptance or deferred payment is due at maturity, whether or not another nominated bank prepaid or purchased before maturity. A confirming bank's undertaking to reimburse another nominated bank is independent of the confirming bank's undertaking to the beneficiary.

d. If a bank is authorized or requested by the issuing bank to confirm a credit but is not prepared to do so, it must inform the issuing bank without delay and may advise the credit without confirmation.

© 2006 International Chamber of Commerce

Article 9

Advising of Credits and Amendments

a. A credit and any amendment may be advised to a beneficiary through an advising bank. An advising bank that is not a confirming bank advises the credit and any amendment without any undertaking to honour or negotiate.

b. By advising the credit or amendment, the advising bank signifies that it has satisfied itself as to the apparent authenticity of the credit or amendment and that the advice accurately reflects the terms and conditions of the credit or amendment received.

c. An advising bank may utilize the services of another bank ("second advising bank") to advise the credit and any amendment to the beneficiary. By advising the credit or amendment, the second advising bank signifies that it has satisfied itself as to the apparent authenticity of the advice it has received and that the advice accurately reflects the terms and conditions of the credit or amendment received.

d. A bank utilizing the services of an advising bank or second advising bank to advise a credit must use the same bank to advise any amendment thereto.

e. If a bank is requested to advise a credit or amendment but elects not to do so, it must so inform, without delay, the bank from which the credit, amendment or advice has been received.

f. If a bank is requested to advise a credit or amendment but cannot satisfy itself as to the apparent authenticity of the credit, the amendment or the advice, it must so inform, without delay, the bank from which the instructions appear to have been received. If the advising bank or second advising bank elects nonetheless to advise the credit or amendment, it must inform the beneficiary or second advising bank that it has not been able to satisfy itself as to the apparent authenticity of the credit, the amendment or the advice.

© 2006 International Chamber of Commerce

Article 10

Amendments

a. Except as otherwise provided by article 38, a credit can neither be amended nor cancelled without the agreement of the issuing bank, the confirming bank, if any, and the beneficiary.

b. An issuing bank is irrevocably bound by an amendment as of the time it issues the amendment. A confirming bank may extend its confirmation to an amendment and will be irrevocably bound as of the time it advises the amendment. A confirming bank may, however, choose to advise an amendment without extending its confirmation and, if so, it must inform the issuing bank without delay and inform the beneficiary in its advice.

c. The terms and conditions of the original credit (or a credit incorporating previously accepted amendments) will remain in force for the beneficiary until the beneficiary communicates its acceptance of the amendment to the bank that advised such amendment. The beneficiary should give notification of acceptance or rejection of an amendment. If the beneficiary fails to give such notification, a presentation that complies with the credit and to any not yet accepted amendment will be deemed to be notification of acceptance by the beneficiary of such amendment. As of that moment the credit will be amended.

d. A bank that advises an amendment should inform the bank from which it received the amendment of any notification of acceptance or rejection.

e. Partial acceptance of an amendment is not allowed and will be deemed to be notification of rejection of the amendment.

f. A provision in an amendment to the effect that the amendment shall enter into force unless rejected by the beneficiary within a certain time shall be disregarded.

© 2006 International Chamber of Commerce

Article 11

Teletransmitted and Pre-Advised Credits and Amendments

a. An authenticated teletransmission of a credit or amendment will be deemed to be the operative credit or amendment, and any subsequent mail confirmation shall be disregarded.

If a teletransmission states "full details to follow" (or words of similar effect), or states that the mail confirmation is to be the operative credit or amendment, then the teletransmission will not be deemed to be the operative credit or amendment. The issuing bank must then issue the operative credit or amendment without delay in terms not inconsistent with the teletransmission.

b. A preliminary advice of the issuance of a credit or amendment ("pre-advice") shall only be sent if the issuing bank is prepared to issue the operative credit or amendment. An issuing bank that sends a pre-advice is irrevocably committed to issue the operative credit or amendment, without delay, in terms not inconsistent with the pre-advice.

Article 12

Nomination

a. Unless a nominated bank is the confirming bank, an authorization to honour or negotiate does not impose any obligation on that nominated bank to honour or negotiate, except when expressly agreed to by that nominated bank and so communicated to the beneficiary.

b. By nominating a bank to accept a draft or incur a deferred payment undertaking, an issuing bank authorizes that nominated bank to prepay or purchase a draft accepted or a deferred payment undertaking incurred by that nominated bank.

c. Receipt or examination and forwarding of documents by a nominated bank that is not a confirming bank does not make that nominated bank liable to honour or negotiate, nor does it constitute honour or negotiation.

© 2006 International Chamber of Commerce

Article 13

Bank-to-Bank Reimbursement Arrangements

a. If a credit states that reimbursement is to be obtained by a nominated bank ("claiming bank") claiming on another party ("reimbursing bank"), the credit must state if the reimbursement is subject to the ICC rules for bank-to-bank reimbursements in effect on the date of issuance of the credit.

b. If a credit does not state that reimbursement is subject to the ICC rules for bank-to-bank reimbursements, the following apply:

i. An issuing bank must provide a reimbursing bank with a reimbursement authorization that conforms with the availability stated in the credit. The reimbursement authorization should not be subject to an expiry date.

ii. A claiming bank shall not be required to supply a reimbursing bank with a certificate of compliance with the terms and conditions of the credit.

iii. An issuing bank will be responsible for any loss of interest, together with any expenses incurred, if reimbursement is not provided on first demand by a reimbursing bank in accordance with the terms and conditions of the credit.

iv. A reimbursing bank's charges are for the account of the issuing bank. However, if the charges are for the account of the beneficiary, it is the responsibility of an issuing bank to so indicate in the credit and in the reimbursement authorization. If a reimbursing bank's charges are for the account of the beneficiary, they shall be deducted from the amount due to a claiming bank when reimbursement is made. If no reimbursement is made, the reimbursing bank's charges remain the obligation of the issuing bank.

c. An issuing bank is not relieved of any of its obligations to provide reimbursement if reimbursement is not made by a reimbursing bank on first demand.

© 2006 International Chamber of Commerce

Article 14

Standard for Examination of Documents

a. A nominated bank acting on its nomination, a confirming bank, if any, and the issuing bank must examine a presentation to determine, on the basis of the documents alone, whether or not the documents appear on their face to constitute a complying presentation.

b. A nominated bank acting on its nomination, a confirming bank, if any, and the issuing bank shall each have a maximum of five banking days following the day of presentation to determine if a presentation is complying. This period is not curtailed or otherwise affected by the occurrence on or after the date of presentation of any expiry date or last day for presentation.

c. A presentation including one or more original transport documents subject to articles 19, 20, 21, 22, 23, 24 or 25 must be made by or on behalf of the beneficiary not later than 21 calendar days after the date of shipment as described in these rules, but in any event not later than the expiry date of the credit.

d. Data in a document, when read in context with the credit, the document itself and international standard banking practice, need not be identical to, but must not conflict with, data in that document, any other stipulated document or the credit.

e. In documents other than the commercial invoice, the description of the goods, services or performance, if stated, may be in general terms not conflicting with their description in the credit.

f. If a credit requires presentation of a document other than a transport document, insurance document or commercial invoice, without stipulating by whom the document is to be issued or its data content, banks will accept the document as presented if its content appears to fulfil the function of the required document and otherwise complies with sub-article 14 (d).

g. A document presented but not required by the credit will be disregarded and may be returned to the presenter.

h. If a credit contains a condition without stipulating the document to indicate compliance with the condition, banks will deem such condition as not stated and will disregard it.

© 2006 International Chamber of Commerce

i. A document may be dated prior to the issuance date of the credit, but must not be dated later than its date of presentation.

j. When the addresses of the beneficiary and the applicant appear in any stipulated document, they need not be the same as those stated in the credit or in any other stipulated document, but must be within the same country as the respective addresses mentioned in the credit. Contact details (telefax, telephone, email and the like) stated as part of the beneficiary's and the applicant's address will be disregarded. However, when the address and contact details of the applicant appear as part of the consignee or notify party details on a transport document subject to articles 19, 20, 21, 22, 23, 24 or 25, they must be as stated in the credit.

k. The shipper or consignor of the goods indicated on any document need not be the beneficiary of the credit.

l. A transport document may be issued by any party other than a carrier, owner, master or charterer provided that the transport document meets the requirements of articles 19, 20, 21, 22, 23 or 24 of these rules.

Article 15

Complying Presentation

a. When an issuing bank determines that a presentation is complying, it must honour.

b. When a confirming bank determines that a presentation is complying, it must honour or negotiate and forward the documents to the issuing bank.

c. When a nominated bank determines that a presentation is complying and honours or negotiates, it must forward the documents to the confirming bank or issuing bank.

© 2006 International Chamber of Commerce

Article 16

Discrepant Documents, Waiver and Notice

a. When a nominated bank acting on its nomination, a confirming bank, if any, or the issuing bank determines that a presentation does not comply, it may refuse to honour or negotiate.

b. When an issuing bank determines that a presentation does not comply, it may in its sole judgement approach the applicant for a waiver of the discrepancies. This does not, however, extend the period mentioned in sub-article 14 (b).

c. When a nominated bank acting on its nomination, a confirming bank, if any, or the issuing bank decides to refuse to honour or negotiate, it must give a single notice to that effect to the presenter.

The notice must state:

i. that the bank is refusing to honour or negotiate; and

ii. each discrepancy in respect of which the bank refuses to honour or negotiate; and

iii. a) that the bank is holding the documents pending further instructions from the presenter; or

b) that the issuing bank is holding the documents until it receives a waiver from the applicant and agrees to accept it, or receives further instructions from the presenter prior to agreeing to accept a waiver; or

c) that the bank is returning the documents; or

d) that the bank is acting in accordance with instructions previously received from the presenter.

d. The notice required in sub-article 16 (c) must be given by telecommunication or, if that is not possible, by other expeditious means no later than the close of the fifth banking day following the day of presentation.

e. A nominated bank acting on its nomination, a confirming bank, if any, or the issuing bank may, after providing notice required by sub-article 16 (c) (iii) (a) or (b), return the documents to the presenter at any time.

© 2006 International Chamber of Commerce

f. If an issuing bank or a confirming bank fails to act in accordance with the provisions of this article, it shall be precluded from claiming that the documents do not constitute a complying presentation.

g. When an issuing bank refuses to honour or a confirming bank refuses to honour or negotiate and has given notice to that effect in accordance with this article, it shall then be entitled to claim a refund, with interest, of any reimbursement made.

Article 17

Original Documents and Copies

a. At least one original of each document stipulated in the credit must be presented.

b. A bank shall treat as an original any document bearing an apparently original signature, mark, stamp, or label of the issuer of the document, unless the document itself indicates that it is not an original.

c. Unless a document indicates otherwise, a bank will also accept a document as original if it:

i. appears to be written, typed, perforated or stamped by the document issuer's hand; or

ii. appears to be on the document issuer's original stationery; or

iii. states that it is original, unless the statement appears not to apply to the document presented.

d. If a credit requires presentation of copies of documents, presentation of either originals or copies is permitted.

e. If a credit requires presentation of multiple documents by using terms such as "in duplicate", "in two fold" or "in two copies", this will be satisfied by the presentation of at least one original and the remaining number in copies, except when the document itself indicates otherwise.

© 2006 International Chamber of Commerce

ARTICLE 18

Commercial Invoice

a. A commercial invoice:

i. must appear to have been issued by the beneficiary (except as provided in article 38);

ii. must be made out in the name of the applicant (except as provided in sub-article 38 (g));

iii. must be made out in the same currency as the credit; and

iv. need not be signed.

b. A nominated bank acting on its nomination, a confirming bank, if any, or the issuing bank may accept a commercial invoice issued for an amount in excess of the amount permitted by the credit, and its decision will be binding upon all parties, provided the bank in question has not honoured or negotiated for an amount in excess of that permitted by the credit.

c. The description of the goods, services or performance in a commercial invoice must correspond with that appearing in the credit.

ARTICLE 19

Transport Document Covering at Least Two Different Modes of Transport

a. A transport document covering at least two different modes of transport (multimodal or combined transport document), however named, must appear to:

i. indicate the name of the carrier and be signed by:

- the carrier or a named agent for or on behalf of the carrier, or
- the master or a named agent for or on behalf of the master.

Any signature by the carrier, master or agent must be identified as that of the carrier, master or agent.

Any signature by an agent must indicate whether the agent has signed for or on behalf of the carrier or for or on behalf of the master.

© 2006 International Chamber of Commerce

ii. indicate that the goods have been dispatched, taken in charge or shipped on board at the place stated in the credit, by:

- pre-printed wording, or
- a stamp or notation indicating the date on which the goods have been dispatched, taken in charge or shipped on board.

The date of issuance of the transport document will be deemed to be the date of dispatch, taking in charge or shipped on board, and the date of shipment. However, if the transport document indicates, by stamp or notation, a date of dispatch, taking in charge or shipped on board, this date will be deemed to be the date of shipment.

iii. indicate the place of dispatch, taking in charge or shipment, and the place of final destination stated in the credit, even if:

a) the transport document states, in addition, a different place of dispatch, taking in charge or shipment or place of final destination, or

b) the transport document contains the indication "intended" or similar qualification in relation to the vessel, port of loading or port of discharge.

iv. be the sole original transport document or, if issued in more than one original, be the full set as indicated on the transport document.

v. contain terms and conditions of carriage or make reference to another source containing the terms and conditions of carriage (short form or blank back transport document). Contents of terms and conditions of carriage will not be examined.

vi. contain no indication that it is subject to a charter party.

b. For the purpose of this article, transhipment means unloading from one means of conveyance and reloading to another means of conveyance (whether or not in different modes of transport) during the carriage from the place of dispatch, taking in charge or shipment to the place of final destination stated in the credit.

c. i. A transport document may indicate that the goods will or may be transhipped provided that the entire carriage is covered by one and the same transport document.

© 2006 International Chamber of Commerce

ii. A transport document indicating that transhipment will or may take place is acceptable, even if the credit prohibits transhipment.

ARTICLE 20

Bill of Lading

a. A bill of lading, however named, must appear to:

i. indicate the name of the carrier and be signed by:

- the carrier or a named agent for or on behalf of the carrier, or
- the master or a named agent for or on behalf of the master.

Any signature by the carrier, master or agent must be identified as that of the carrier, master or agent.

Any signature by an agent must indicate whether the agent has signed for or on behalf of the carrier or for or on behalf of the master.

ii. indicate that the goods have been shipped on board a named vessel at the port of loading stated in the credit by:

- pre-printed wording, or
- an on board notation indicating the date on which the goods have been shipped on board.

The date of issuance of the bill of lading will be deemed to be the date of shipment unless the bill of lading contains an on board notation indicating the date of shipment, in which case the date stated in the on board notation will be deemed to be the date of shipment.

If the bill of lading contains the indication "intended vessel" or similar qualification in relation to the name of the vessel, an on board notation indicating the date of shipment and the name of the actual vessel is required.

iii. indicate shipment from the port of loading to the port of discharge stated in the credit.

© 2006 International Chamber of Commerce

If the bill of lading does not indicate the port of loading stated in the credit as the port of loading, or if it contains the indication "intended" or similar qualification in relation to the port of loading, an on board notation indicating the port of loading as stated in the credit, the date of shipment and the name of the vessel is required. This provision applies even when loading on board or shipment on a named vessel is indicated by pre-printed wording on the bill of lading.

iv. be the sole original bill of lading or, if issued in more than one original, be the full set as indicated on the bill of lading.

v. contain terms and conditions of carriage or make reference to another source containing the terms and conditions of carriage (short form or blank back bill of lading). Contents of terms and conditions of carriage will not be examined.

vi. contain no indication that it is subject to a charter party.

b. For the purpose of this article, transhipment means unloading from one vessel and reloading to another vessel during the carriage from the port of loading to the port of discharge stated in the credit.

c. **i.** A bill of lading may indicate that the goods will or may be transhipped provided that the entire carriage is covered by one and the same bill of lading.

ii. A bill of lading indicating that transhipment will or may take place is acceptable, even if the credit prohibits transhipment, if the goods have been shipped in a container, trailer or LASH barge as evidenced by the bill of lading.

d. Clauses in a bill of lading stating that the carrier reserves the right to tranship will be disregarded.

© 2006 International Chamber of Commerce

Article 21

Non-Negotiable Sea Waybill

a. A non-negotiable sea waybill, however named, must appear to:

i. indicate the name of the carrier and be signed by:

- the carrier or a named agent for or on behalf of the carrier, or
- the master or a named agent for or on behalf of the master.

Any signature by the carrier, master or agent must be identified as that of the carrier, master or agent.

Any signature by an agent must indicate whether the agent has signed for or on behalf of the carrier or for or on behalf of the master.

ii. indicate that the goods have been shipped on board a named vessel at the port of loading stated in the credit by:

- pre-printed wording, or
- an on board notation indicating the date on which the goods have been shipped on board.

The date of issuance of the non-negotiable sea waybill will be deemed to be the date of shipment unless the non-negotiable sea waybill contains an on board notation indicating the date of shipment, in which case the date stated in the on board notation will be deemed to be the date of shipment.

If the non-negotiable sea waybill contains the indication "intended vessel" or similar qualification in relation to the name of the vessel, an on board notation indicating the date of shipment and the name of the actual vessel is required.

© 2006 International Chamber of Commerce

iii. indicate shipment from the port of loading to the port of discharge stated in the credit.

If the non-negotiable sea waybill does not indicate the port of loading stated in the credit as the port of loading, or if it contains the indication "intended" or similar qualification in relation to the port of loading, an on board notation indicating the port of loading as stated in the credit, the date of shipment and the name of the vessel is required. This provision applies even when loading on board or shipment on a named vessel is indicated by pre-printed wording on the non-negotiable sea waybill.

iv. be the sole original non-negotiable sea waybill or, if issued in more than one original, be the full set as indicated on the non-negotiable sea waybill.

v. contain terms and conditions of carriage or make reference to another source containing the terms and conditions of carriage (short form or blank back non-negotiable sea waybill). Contents of terms and conditions of carriage will not be examined.

vi. contain no indication that it is subject to a charter party.

b. For the purpose of this article, transhipment means unloading from one vessel and reloading to another vessel during the carriage from the port of loading to the port of discharge stated in the credit.

c. **i.** A non-negotiable sea waybill may indicate that the goods will or may be transhipped provided that the entire carriage is covered by one and the same non-negotiable sea waybill.

ii. A non-negotiable sea waybill indicating that transhipment will or may take place is acceptable, even if the credit prohibits transhipment, if the goods have been shipped in a container, trailer or LASH barge as evidenced by the non-negotiable sea waybill.

d. Clauses in a non-negotiable sea waybill stating that the carrier reserves the right to tranship will be disregarded.

© 2006 International Chamber of Commerce

Article 22

Charter Party Bill of Lading

a. A bill of lading, however named, containing an indication that it is subject to a charter party (charter party bill of lading), must appear to:

i. be signed by:

- the master or a named agent for or on behalf of the master, or
- the owner or a named agent for or on behalf of the owner, or
- the charterer or a named agent for or on behalf of the charterer.

Any signature by the master, owner, charterer or agent must be identified as that of the master, owner, charterer or agent.

Any signature by an agent must indicate whether the agent has signed for or on behalf of the master, owner or charterer.

An agent signing for or on behalf of the owner or charterer must indicate the name of the owner or charterer.

ii. indicate that the goods have been shipped on board a named vessel at the port of loading stated in the credit by:

- pre-printed wording, or
- an on board notation indicating the date on which the goods have been shipped on board.

The date of issuance of the charter party bill of lading will be deemed to be the date of shipment unless the charter party bill of lading contains an on board notation indicating the date of shipment, in which case the date stated in the on board notation will be deemed to be the date of shipment.

iii. indicate shipment from the port of loading to the port of discharge stated in the credit. The port of discharge may also be shown as a range of ports or a geographical area, as stated in the credit.

iv. be the sole original charter party bill of lading or, if issued in more than one original, be the full set as indicated on the charter party bill of lading.

© 2006 International Chamber of Commerce

b. A bank will not examine charter party contracts, even if they are required to be presented by the terms of the credit.

Article 23

Air Transport Document

a. An air transport document, however named, must appear to:

i. indicate the name of the carrier and be signed by:

- the carrier, or
- a named agent for or on behalf of the carrier.

Any signature by the carrier or agent must be identified as that of the carrier or agent.

Any signature by an agent must indicate that the agent has signed for or on behalf of the carrier.

ii. indicate that the goods have been accepted for carriage.

iii. indicate the date of issuance. This date will be deemed to be the date of shipment unless the air transport document contains a specific notation of the actual date of shipment, in which case the date stated in the notation will be deemed to be the date of shipment.

Any other information appearing on the air transport document relative to the flight number and date will not be considered in determining the date of shipment.

iv. indicate the airport of departure and the airport of destination stated in the credit.

v. be the original for consignor or shipper, even if the credit stipulates a full set of originals.

vi. contain terms and conditions of carriage or make reference to another source containing the terms and conditions of carriage. Contents of terms and conditions of carriage will not be examined.

b. For the purpose of this article, transhipment means unloading from one aircraft and reloading to another aircraft during the carriage from the airport of departure to the airport of destination stated in the credit.

© 2006 International Chamber of Commerce

c. **i.** An air transport document may indicate that the goods will or may be transhipped, provided that the entire carriage is covered by one and the same air transport document.

ii. An air transport document indicating that transhipment will or may take place is acceptable, even if the credit prohibits transhipment.

ARTICLE 24

Road, Rail or Inland Waterway Transport Documents

a. A road, rail or inland waterway transport document, however named, must appear to:

i. indicate the name of the carrier and:

- be signed by the carrier or a named agent for or on behalf of the carrier, or
- indicate receipt of the goods by signature, stamp or notation by the carrier or a named agent for or on behalf of the carrier.

Any signature, stamp or notation of receipt of the goods by the carrier or agent must be identified as that of the carrier or agent.

Any signature, stamp or notation of receipt of the goods by the agent must indicate that the agent has signed or acted for or on behalf of the carrier.

If a rail transport document does not identify the carrier, any signature or stamp of the railway company will be accepted as evidence of the document being signed by the carrier.

ii. indicate the date of shipment or the date the goods have been received for shipment, dispatch or carriage at the place stated in the credit. Unless the transport document contains a dated reception stamp, an indication of the date of receipt or a date of shipment, the date of issuance of the transport document will be deemed to be the date of shipment.

iii. indicate the place of shipment and the place of destination stated in the credit.

© 2006 International Chamber of Commerce

b. **i.** A road transport document must appear to be the original for consignor or shipper or bear no marking indicating for whom the document has been prepared.

ii. A rail transport document marked "duplicate" will be accepted as an original.

iii. A rail or inland waterway transport document will be accepted as an original whether marked as an original or not.

c. In the absence of an indication on the transport document as to the number of originals issued, the number presented will be deemed to constitute a full set.

d. For the purpose of this article, transhipment means unloading from one means of conveyance and reloading to another means of conveyance, within the same mode of transport, during the carriage from the place of shipment, dispatch or carriage to the place of destination stated in the credit.

e. **i.** A road, rail or inland waterway transport document may indicate that the goods will or may be transhipped provided that the entire carriage is covered by one and the same transport document.

ii. A road, rail or inland waterway transport document indicating that transhipment will or may take place is acceptable, even if the credit prohibits transhipment.

Article 25

Courier Receipt, Post Receipt or Certificate of Posting

a. A courier receipt, however named, evidencing receipt of goods for transport, must appear to:

i. indicate the name of the courier service and be stamped or signed by the named courier service at the place from which the credit states the goods are to be shipped; and

ii. indicate a date of pickup or of receipt or wording to this effect. This date will be deemed to be the date of shipment.

© 2006 International Chamber of Commerce

b. A requirement that courier charges are to be paid or prepaid may be satisfied by a transport document issued by a courier service evidencing that courier charges are for the account of a party other than the consignee.

c. A post receipt or certificate of posting, however named, evidencing receipt of goods for transport, must appear to be stamped or signed and dated at the place from which the credit states the goods are to be shipped. This date will be deemed to be the date of shipment.

Article 26

"On Deck", "Shipper's Load and Count", "Said by Shipper to Contain" and Charges Additional to Freight

a. A transport document must not indicate that the goods are or will be loaded on deck. A clause on a transport document stating that the goods may be loaded on deck is acceptable.

b. A transport document bearing a clause such as "shipper's load and count" and "said by shipper to contain" is acceptable.

c. A transport document may bear a reference, by stamp or otherwise, to charges additional to the freight.

Article 27

Clean Transport Document

A bank will only accept a clean transport document. A clean transport document is one bearing no clause or notation expressly declaring a defective condition of the goods or their packaging. The word "clean" need not appear on a transport document, even if a credit has a requirement for that transport document to be "clean on board".

© 2006 International Chamber of Commerce

Article 28

Insurance Document and Coverage

a. An insurance document, such as an insurance policy, an insurance certificate or a declaration under an open cover, must appear to be issued and signed by an insurance company, an underwriter or their agents or their proxies.

Any signature by an agent or proxy must indicate whether the agent or proxy has signed for or on behalf of the insurance company or underwriter.

b. When the insurance document indicates that it has been issued in more than one original, all originals must be presented.

c. Cover notes will not be accepted.

d. An insurance policy is acceptable in lieu of an insurance certificate or a declaration under an open cover.

e. The date of the insurance document must be no later than the date of shipment, unless it appears from the insurance document that the cover is effective from a date not later than the date of shipment.

f. **i.** The insurance document must indicate the amount of insurance coverage and be in the same currency as the credit.

ii. A requirement in the credit for insurance coverage to be for a percentage of the value of the goods, of the invoice value or similar is deemed to be the minimum amount of coverage required.

If there is no indication in the credit of the insurance coverage required, the amount of insurance coverage must be at least 110% of the CIF or CIP value of the goods.

When the CIF or CIP value cannot be determined from the documents, the amount of insurance coverage must be calculated on the basis of the amount for which honour or negotiation is requested or the gross value of the goods as shown on the invoice, whichever is greater.

© 2006 International Chamber of Commerce

iii. The insurance document must indicate that risks are covered at least between the place of taking in charge or shipment and the place of discharge or final destination as stated in the credit.

g. A credit should state the type of insurance required and, if any, the additional risks to be covered. An insurance document will be accepted without regard to any risks that are not covered if the credit uses imprecise terms such as "usual risks" or "customary risks".

h. When a credit requires insurance against "all risks" and an insurance document is presented containing any "all risks" notation or clause, whether or not bearing the heading "all risks", the insurance document will be accepted without regard to any risks stated to be excluded.

i. An insurance document may contain reference to any exclusion clause.

j. An insurance document may indicate that the cover is subject to a franchise or excess (deductible).

Article 29

Extension of Expiry Date or Last Day for Presentation

a. If the expiry date of a credit or the last day for presentation falls on a day when the bank to which presentation is to be made is closed for reasons other than those referred to in article 36, the expiry date or the last day for presentation, as the case may be, will be extended to the first following banking day.

b. If presentation is made on the first following banking day, a nominated bank must provide the issuing bank or confirming bank with a statement on its covering schedule that the presentation was made within the time limits extended in accordance with sub-article 29 (a).

c. The latest date for shipment will not be extended as a result of sub-article 29 (a).

© 2006 International Chamber of Commerce

Article 30

Tolerance in Credit Amount, Quantity and Unit Prices

a. The words "about" or "approximately" used in connection with the amount of the credit or the quantity or the unit price stated in the credit are to be construed as allowing a tolerance not to exceed 10% more or 10% less than the amount, the quantity or the unit price to which they refer.

b. A tolerance not to exceed 5% more or 5% less than the quantity of the goods is allowed, provided the credit does not state the quantity in terms of a stipulated number of packing units or individual items and the total amount of the drawings does not exceed the amount of the credit.

c. Even when partial shipments are not allowed, a tolerance not to exceed 5% less than the amount of the credit is allowed, provided that the quantity of the goods, if stated in the credit, is shipped in full and a unit price, if stated in the credit, is not reduced or that sub-article 30 (b) is not applicable. This tolerance does not apply when the credit stipulates a specific tolerance or uses the expressions referred to in sub-article 30 (a).

Article 31

Partial Drawings or Shipments

a. Partial drawings or shipments are allowed.

b. A presentation consisting of more than one set of transport documents evidencing shipment commencing on the same means of conveyance and for the same journey, provided they indicate the same destination, will not be regarded as covering a partial shipment, even if they indicate different dates of shipment or different ports of loading, places of taking in charge or dispatch. If the presentation consists of more than one set of transport documents, the latest date of shipment as evidenced on any of the sets of transport documents will be regarded as the date of shipment.

© 2006 International Chamber of Commerce

A presentation consisting of one or more sets of transport documents evidencing shipment on more than one means of conveyance within the same mode of transport will be regarded as covering a partial shipment, even if the means of conveyance leave on the same day for the same destination.

c. A presentation consisting of more than one courier receipt, post receipt or certificate of posting will not be regarded as a partial shipment if the courier receipts, post receipts or certificates of posting appear to have been stamped or signed by the same courier or postal service at the same place and date and for the same destination.

ARTICLE 32

Instalment Drawings or Shipments

If a drawing or shipment by instalments within given periods is stipulated in the credit and any instalment is not drawn or shipped within the period allowed for that instalment, the credit ceases to be available for that and any subsequent instalment.

ARTICLE 33

Hours of Presentation

A bank has no obligation to accept a presentation outside of its banking hours.

ARTICLE 34

Disclaimer on Effectiveness of Documents

A bank assumes no liability or responsibility for the form, sufficiency, accuracy, genuineness, falsification or legal effect of any document, or for the general or particular conditions stipulated in a document or superimposed thereon; nor does it assume any liability or responsibility for the description, quantity, weight, quality, condition, packing, delivery, value or existence of the goods, services or other performance represented by any document, or for the good faith or acts or omissions, solvency, performance or standing of the consignor, the carrier, the forwarder, the consignee or the insurer of the goods or any other person.

© 2006 International Chamber of Commerce

Article 35

Disclaimer on Transmission and Translation

A bank assumes no liability or responsibility for the consequences arising out of delay, loss in transit, mutilation or other errors arising in the transmission of any messages or delivery of letters or documents, when such messages, letters or documents are transmitted or sent according to the requirements stated in the credit, or when the bank may have taken the initiative in the choice of the delivery service in the absence of such instructions in the credit.

If a nominated bank determines that a presentation is complying and forwards the documents to the issuing bank or confirming bank, whether or not the nominated bank has honoured or negotiated, an issuing bank or confirming bank must honour or negotiate, or reimburse that nominated bank, even when the documents have been lost in transit between the nominated bank and the issuing bank or confirming bank, or between the confirming bank and the issuing bank.

A bank assumes no liability or responsibility for errors in translation or interpretation of technical terms and may transmit credit terms without translating them.

Article 36

Force Majeure

A bank assumes no liability or responsibility for the consequences arising out of the interruption of its business by Acts of God, riots, civil commotions, insurrections, wars, acts of terrorism, or by any strikes or lockouts or any other causes beyond its control.

A bank will not, upon resumption of its business, honour or negotiate under a credit that expired during such interruption of its business.

© 2006 International Chamber of Commerce

ARTICLE 37

Disclaimer for Acts of an Instructed Party

a. A bank utilizing the services of another bank for the purpose of giving effect to the instructions of the applicant does so for the account and at the risk of the applicant.

b. An issuing bank or advising bank assumes no liability or responsibility should the instructions it transmits to another bank not be carried out, even if it has taken the initiative in the choice of that other bank.

c. A bank instructing another bank to perform services is liable for any commissions, fees, costs or expenses ("charges") incurred by that bank in connection with its instructions.

If a credit states that charges are for the account of the beneficiary and charges cannot be collected or deducted from proceeds, the issuing bank remains liable for payment of charges.

A credit or amendment should not stipulate that the advising to a beneficiary is conditional upon the receipt by the advising bank or second advising bank of its charges.

d. The applicant shall be bound by and liable to indemnify a bank against all obligations and responsibilities imposed by foreign laws and usages.

ARTICLE 38

Transferable Credits

a. A bank is under no obligation to transfer a credit except to the extent and in the manner expressly consented to by that bank.

b. For the purpose of this article:

Transferable credit means a credit that specifically states it is "transferable". A transferable credit may be made available in whole or in part to another beneficiary ("second beneficiary") at the request of the beneficiary ("first beneficiary").

Transferring bank means a nominated bank that transfers the credit or, in a credit available with any bank, a bank that is specifically authorized by the issuing bank to transfer and that transfers the credit. An issuing bank may be a transferring bank.

© 2006 International Chamber of Commerce

Transferred credit means a credit that has been made available by the transferring bank to a second beneficiary.

c. Unless otherwise agreed at the time of transfer, all charges (such as commissions, fees, costs or expenses) incurred in respect of a transfer must be paid by the first beneficiary.

d. A credit may be transferred in part to more than one second beneficiary provided partial drawings or shipments are allowed.

A transferred credit cannot be transferred at the request of a second beneficiary to any subsequent beneficiary. The first beneficiary is not considered to be a subsequent beneficiary.

e. Any request for transfer must indicate if and under what conditions amendments may be advised to the second beneficiary. The transferred credit must clearly indicate those conditions.

f. If a credit is transferred to more than one second beneficiary, rejection of an amendment by one or more second beneficiary does not invalidate the acceptance by any other second beneficiary, with respect to which the transferred credit will be amended accordingly. For any second beneficiary that rejected the amendment, the transferred credit will remain unamended.

g. The transferred credit must accurately reflect the terms and conditions of the credit, including confirmation, if any, with the exception of:

- the amount of the credit,
- any unit price stated therein,
- the expiry date,
- the period for presentation, or
- the latest shipment date or given period for shipment,

any or all of which may be reduced or curtailed.

The percentage for which insurance cover must be effected may be increased to provide the amount of cover stipulated in the credit or these articles.

© 2006 International Chamber of Commerce

The name of the first beneficiary may be substituted for that of the applicant in the credit.

If the name of the applicant is specifically required by the credit to appear in any document other than the invoice, such requirement must be reflected in the transferred credit.

h. The first beneficiary has the right to substitute its own invoice and draft, if any, for those of a second beneficiary for an amount not in excess of that stipulated in the credit, and upon such substitution the first beneficiary can draw under the credit for the difference, if any, between its invoice and the invoice of a second beneficiary.

i. If the first beneficiary is to present its own invoice and draft, if any, but fails to do so on first demand, or if the invoices presented by the first beneficiary create discrepancies that did not exist in the presentation made by the second beneficiary and the first beneficiary fails to correct them on first demand, the transferring bank has the right to present the documents as received from the second beneficiary to the issuing bank, without further responsibility to the first beneficiary.

j. The first beneficiary may, in its request for transfer, indicate that honour or negotiation is to be effected to a second beneficiary at the place to which the credit has been transferred, up to and including the expiry date of the credit. This is without prejudice to the right of the first beneficiary in accordance with sub-article 38 (h).

k. Presentation of documents by or on behalf of a second beneficiary must be made to the transferring bank.

ARTICLE 39

Assignment of Proceeds

The fact that a credit is not stated to be transferable shall not affect the right of the beneficiary to assign any proceeds to which it may be or may become entitled under the credit, in accordance with the provisions of applicable law. This article relates only to the assignment of proceeds and not to the assignment of the right to perform under the credit.

© 2006 International Chamber of Commerce

Supplement for Electronic Presentation
Version 1.1

Introduction

The official name for this publication is "Supplement to the Uniform Customs and Practice for Documentary Credits for Electronic Presentation (Version 1.1)". It uses the acronym "eUCP".

During the course of drafting UCP 600, ICC national committees indicated that, due to the limited usage of eUCP Version 1.0, the eUCP should remain as a supplement to the UCP. Version 1.1 has, therefore, been updated solely to reflect the changes made in UCP with regard to terminology and style of presentation.

The eUCP continues to provide definitions permitting UCP 600 terminology accommodating the electronic presentation of the equivalent of paper documents and providing necessary rules to allow both sets of rules to work together. The eUCP allows for presentation electronically or for a mixture of paper documents and electronic presentation.

It is important for the eUCP reader to understand that many articles of the UCP are not impacted by the presentation of the electronic equivalent of paper documents and do not require any changes to accommodate electronic presentation.

When read together, the UCP and the eUCP provide the necessary rules for electronic presentation and are broad enough to anticipate developing practice in this area. Where specific words or phrases used in the UCP are defined in the eUCP, these definitions, unless otherwise stated, apply wherever the terms appear in the UCP.

eUCP Version 1.1 is specific to UCP 600 and, if necessary, may have to be revised as technologies develop, perhaps prior to the next revision of the UCP. For that purpose, the eUCP is issued in version numbers that will allow for a revision and subsequent version if the need arises.

The eUCP has been specifically drafted to be independent of specific technologies and developing electronic commerce systems, i.e., it does not address specific technologies or systems necessary to facilitate electronic presentation. These technologies are evolving, and it is left to the parties to the credit to agree on the technology or systems to be used for presentation of electronic records in compliance with the requirements of the eUCP.

© 2006 International Chamber of Commerce

The eUCP has been created to meet the demands of the market for the presentation of electronic documents. The market has created a higher standard in anticipation of increased processing efficiencies when the electronic equivalents of paper documents are presented. In anticipation of this demand and to meet market expectations, several changes to the standards established by the UCP have been deemed necessary for an electronic presentation. These changes are consistent with current practice and the expectations of the marketplace.

All of the articles of eUCP Version 1.1 are consistent with UCP 600 except as they relate specifically to electronic presentations. Where necessary, changes have been made to address the unique issues related to presentation of the electronic equivalent of paper documents.

In order to avoid confusion between the articles of the UCP and those of the eUCP, the eUCP articles are numbered with an "e" preceding each article number.

Gary Collyer
Corporate Director,
ABN AMRO Bank N.V., London, UK
and Technical Adviser to the ICC Commission
on Banking Technique and Practice

November 2006

© 2006 International Chamber of Commerce

ARTICLE e1

Scope of the eUCP

a. The Supplement to the Uniform Customs and Practice for Documentary Credits for Electronic Presentation ("eUCP") supplements the Uniform Customs and Practice for Documentary Credits (2007 Revision ICC Publication No. 600) ("UCP") in order to accommodate presentation of electronic records alone or in combination with paper documents.

b. The eUCP shall apply as a supplement to the UCP where the credit indicates that it is subject to eUCP.

c. This version is Version 1.1. A credit must indicate the applicable version of the eUCP. If it does not do so, it is subject to the version in effect on the date the credit is issued or, if made subject to eUCP by an amendment accepted by the beneficiary, on the date of that amendment.

ARTICLE e2

Relationship of the eUCP to the UCP

a. A credit subject to the eUCP ("eUCP credit") is also subject to the UCP without express incorporation of the UCP.

b. Where the eUCP applies, its provisions shall prevail to the extent that they would produce a result different from the application of the UCP.

c. If an eUCP credit allows the beneficiary to choose between presentation of paper documents or electronic records and it chooses to present only paper documents, the UCP alone shall apply to that presentation. If only paper documents are permitted under an eUCP credit, the UCP alone shall apply.

© 2006 International Chamber of Commerce

Article e3

Definitions

a. Where the following terms are used in the UCP, for the purposes of applying the UCP to an electronic record presented under an eUCP credit, the term:

i. **appear on their face** and the like shall apply to examination of the data content of an electronic record.

ii. **document** shall include an electronic record.

iii. **place for presentation** of electronic records means an electronic address.

iv. **sign** and the like shall include an electronic signature.

v. **superimposed**, **notation** or **stamped** means data content whose supplementary character is apparent in an electronic record.

b. The following terms used in the eUCP shall have the following meanings:

i. **electronic record** means

- data created, generated, sent, communicated, received or stored by electronic means
- that is capable of being authenticated as to the apparent identity of a sender and the apparent source of the data contained in it, and as to whether it has remained complete and unaltered, and
- is capable of being examined for compliance with the terms and conditions of the eUCP credit.

ii. **electronic signature** means a data process attached to or logically associated with an electronic record and executed or adopted by a person in order to identify that person and to indicate that person's authentication of the electronic record.

iii. **format** means the data organization in which the electronic record is expressed or to which it refers.

iv. **paper document** means a document in a traditional paper form.

© 2006 International Chamber of Commerce

v. **received** means the time when an electronic record enters the information system of the applicable recipient in a form capable of being accepted by that system. Any acknowledgement of receipt does not imply acceptance or refusal of the electronic record under an eUCP credit.

Article e4

Format

An eUCP credit must specify the formats in which electronic records are to be presented. If the format of the electronic record is not so specified, it may be presented in any format.

Article e5

Presentation

a. An eUCP credit allowing presentation of:

i. electronic records must state a place for presentation of the electronic records.

ii. both electronic records and paper documents must also state a place for presentation of the paper documents.

b. Electronic records may be presented separately and need not be presented at the same time.

c. If an eUCP credit allows for presentation of one or more electronic records, the beneficiary is responsible for providing a notice to the bank to which presentation is made signifying when the presentation is complete. The notice of completeness may be given as an electronic record or paper document and must identify the eUCP credit to which it relates. Presentation is deemed not to have been made if the beneficiary's notice is not received.

d. **i.** Each presentation of an electronic record and the presentation of paper documents under an eUCP credit must identify the eUCP credit under which it is presented.

ii. A presentation not so identified may be treated as not received.

© 2006 International Chamber of Commerce

e. If the bank to which presentation is to be made is open but its system is unable to receive a transmitted electronic record on the stipulated expiry date and/or the last day of the period of time after the date of shipment for presentation, as the case may be, the bank will be deemed to be closed and the date for presentation and/or the expiry date shall be extended to the first following banking day on which such bank is able to receive an electronic record. If the only electronic record remaining to be presented is the notice of completeness, it may be given by telecommunications or by paper document and will be deemed timely, provided that it is sent before the bank is able to receive an electronic record.

f. An electronic record that cannot be authenticated is deemed not to have been presented.

Article e6

Examination

a. If an electronic record contains a hyperlink to an external system or a presentation indicates that the electronic record may be examined by reference to an external system, the electronic record at the hyperlink or the referenced system shall be deemed to be the electronic record to be examined. The failure of the indicated system to provide access to the required electronic record at the time of examination shall constitute a discrepancy.

b. The forwarding of electronic records by a nominated bank pursuant to its nomination signifies that it has satisfied itself as to the apparent authenticity of the electronic records.

c. The inability of the issuing bank, or confirming bank, if any, to examine an electronic record in a format required by the eUCP credit or, if no format is required, to examine it in the format presented is not a basis for refusal.

© 2006 International Chamber of Commerce

ARTICLE e7

Notice of Refusal

a. **i.** The time period for the examination of documents commences on the banking day following the banking day on which the beneficiary's notice of completeness is received.

ii. If the time for presentation of documents or the notice of completeness is extended, the time for the examination of documents commences on the first following banking day on which the bank to which presentation is to be made is able to receive the notice of completeness.

b. If an issuing bank, the confirming bank, if any, or a nominated bank acting on their behalf, provides a notice of refusal of a presentation which includes electronic records and does not receive instructions from the party to which notice of refusal is given within 30 calendar days from the date the notice of refusal is given for the disposition of the electronic records, the bank shall return any paper documents not previously returned to the presenter but may dispose of the electronic records in any manner deemed appropriate without any responsibility.

ARTICLE e8

Originals and Copies

Any requirement of the UCP or an eUCP credit for presentation of one or more originals or copies of an electronic record is satisfied by the presentation of one electronic record.

ARTICLE e9

Date of Issuance

Unless an electronic record contains a specific date of issuance, the date on which it appears to have been sent by the issuer is deemed to be the date of issuance. The date of receipt will be deemed to be the date it was sent if no other date is apparent.

© 2006 International Chamber of Commerce

Article e10

Transport

If an electronic record evidencing transport does not indicate a date of shipment or dispatch, the date of issuance of the electronic record will be deemed to be the date of shipment or dispatch. However, if the electronic record bears a notation that evidences the date of shipment or dispatch, the date of the notation will be deemed to be the date of shipment or dispatch. A notation showing additional data content need not be separately signed or otherwise authenticated.

Article e11

Corruption of an Electronic Record After Presentation

a. If an electronic record that has been received by the issuing bank, confirming bank, or another nominated bank appears to have been corrupted, the bank may inform the presenter and may request that the electronic record be re-presented.

b. If the bank requests that an electronic record be re-presented:

i. the time for examination is suspended and resumes when the presenter re-presents the electronic record; and

ii. if the nominated bank is not the confirming bank, it must provide the issuing bank and any confirming bank with notice of the request for re-presentation and inform it of the suspension; but

iii. if the same electronic record is not re-presented within thirty (30) calendar days, the bank may treat the electronic record as not presented, and

iv. any deadlines are not extended.

© 2006 International Chamber of Commerce

Article e12

Additional Disclaimer of Liability for Presentation of Electronic Records under eUCP

By satisfying itself as to the apparent authenticity of an electronic record, banks assume no liability for the identity of the sender, source of the information or its complete and unaltered character other than that which is apparent in the electronic record received by the use of a commercially acceptable data process for the receipt, authentication and identification of electronic records.

© 2006 International Chamber of Commerce

Acknowledgements

ICC would like to express its appreciation to those members of ICC national committees who put in countless hours reviewing the drafts of the UCP. In addition, a special note of thanks is due to the UCP Consulting Group, which served as an advisory body to the UCP Drafting Group during the course of the UCP revision. The names of Consulting Group members are listed below.

UCP CONSULTING GROUP

Co-chairs

Carlo di Ninni, Associazione Bancaria Italiana, Italy;

John Turnbull, Sumitomo Mitsui Banking Corporation, UK.

Members

Georges Affaki, BNP Paribas, France;

Cveta Andjelkovic, ICC Serbia, Serbia;

Pavel Andrle, ICC Czech Republic, Czech Republic;

Ahsan Aziz, Standard Chartered Bank, Pakistan;

Laurence Bacon, Export Bureaux, Ireland;

Egil Bakken, DNB Nor Bank, Norway;

Rafaél Balbuena Tébar, Balbuena Lawyers, Spain;

James Barnes, Baker & McKenzie, USA;

Rolf J. Breisig, Commerzbank AG, Germany;

Mohammad M. Burjaq, ICC Jordan, Jordan;

James Byrne, Institute of International Banking Law & Practice, USA;

William Cameron, Owen Consulting, Canada;

Dong Heon Chae, Yoon Yang Kim Shin & Yu, Republic of Korea;

Kim Chalmer, A.P. Møller – Mærsk A/S, Denmark;

Gabriel Chami, Bank Audi SAL, Lebanon;

Jin Chen, Industrial and Commercial Bank of China, P.R. China;

Xavier Conti, FFSA, France;

Abdelmalek Dahmani, FIATA, Switzerland;

© 2006 International Chamber of Commerce

Charles Debattista, Institute of Maritime Faculty of Law, UK;
King Tak Fung, Dibb Lupton Alsop, Hong Kong;
K.S. Harshan, The Federal Bank Ltd, India;
Wolfgang Heiter, Deutsche Bank AG, Germany;
Heinz A. Hertl, ICC Austria (Advisor), Austria;
Reinhard Längerich, Nordea Trade Finance (Retired), Denmark;
T.O. Lee, T.O. Lee Consultants Ltd, Canada;
Haifeng Li, ICC China, P.R. China;
Angelo Luiz Lunardi, Edicoes Aduaneiras Ltd, Brazil;
Antonio Maximiano Nicoletti, Spot Training Consultoria e Treinamento Ltda, Brazil;
Dimitris Paleologos, National Bank of Greece, Greece;
Jorge Luis Riva, Raschi y Riva, Argentina;
Saul Daniel Rumeser, P.T. Iradat Consultant, Indonesia;
Marco A. Sangaletti, FIATA, Switzerland;
Donald Smith, Norman Technologies, USA;
Pradeep Taneja, BankMuscat International, Bahrain;
Hennie van Diemen, ING Nederland/Divisie Operations & IT/SC B&CM, Netherlands;
Luc Volkaert, Bolero International Ltd, UK;
Marianne Wabnik, SEB Merchant Banking, Sweden.

© 2006 International Chamber of Commerce

Notes

ICC at a Glance

ICC is the world business organization, a representative body that speaks with authority on behalf of enterprises from all sectors in every part of the world.

The fundamental mission of ICC is to promote trade and investment across frontiers and help business corporations meet the challenges and opportunities of globalization. Its conviction that trade is a powerful force for peace and prosperity dates from the organization's origins early in the last century. The small group of far-sighted business leaders who founded ICC called themselves "the merchants of peace".

Because its member companies and associations are themselves engaged in international business, ICC has unrivalled authority in making rules that govern the conduct of business across borders. Although these rules are voluntary, they are observed in countless thousands of transactions every day and have become part of the fabric of international trade.

ICC also provides essential services, foremost among them the ICC International Court of Arbitration, the world's leading arbitral institution. Another service is the World Chambers Federation, ICC's worldwide network of chambers of commerce, fostering interaction and exchange of chamber best practice.

Within a year of the creation of the United Nations, ICC was granted consultative status at the highest level with the UN and its specialized agencies.

Business leaders and experts drawn from the ICC membership establish the business stance on broad issues of trade and investment policy as well as on vital technical and sectoral subjects. These include financial services, information technologies, telecommunications, marketing ethics, the environment, transportation, competition law and intellectual property.

ICC was founded in 1919. Today it groups thousands of member companies and associations from over 130 countries. National committees work with their members to address the concerns of business in their countries and convey to their governments the business views formulated by ICC.

Some ICC Specialized Divisions

- ICC International Court of Arbitration (Paris)
- ICC International Centre for Expertise (Paris)
- ICC World Chambers Federation (Paris)
- ICC Institute of World Business Law (Paris)
- ICC Centre for Maritime Co-operation (London)
- ICC Commercial Crime Services (London)
- ICC Services *(ICC affiliate*, Paris)

  - **Events Department**

ICC's programme of conferences and seminars is the essential channel for passing on the world business organization's expertise to a wider audience.

ICC Events, a Department of ICC Services, spotlights policy issues of direct concern to business such as banking techniques and practices, e-business, IT and telecoms, piracy and counterfeiting.

ICC Events also runs training courses on international arbitration and negotiating international contracts for business-people, corporate counsel, lawyers and legal practitioners involved in international trade.

  - **Publications Department**

ICC Publications Department is committed to offering the best resources on business and trade for the international community.

The content of ICC publications is derived from the work of ICC commissions, institutions and individual international experts. The specialized list covers a range of topics including international banking, international trade reference and terms (Incoterms), law and arbitration, counterfeiting and fraud, model commercial contracts and environmental issues.

Source Products for Global Business

ICC's specialized list of publications covers a range of topics including international banking, international trade reference and terms (Incoterms), law and arbitration, counterfeiting and fraud, model commercial contracts and environmental issues.

ICC products are available from ICC National Committees, which exist in over 80 countries around the world. Contact details for a National Committee in your country are available at www.iccwbo.org

Publications are available in both traditional and electronic formats from the ICC Business Bookstore at www.iccbooks.com

ICC SERVICES

Publications Department

38, cours Albert ler
75008 Paris, France

Tel +33 1 4953 2923
Fax +33 1 4953 2902
email pub@iccwbo.org

ICC

International Chamber of Commerce

The world business organization